PIER 39

HARASSMENT OF
SEA LIONS IS
A VIOLATION OF
THE MARINE
MAMMAL
PROTECTION ACT
NO DOCKING

Wildlife
in the City

By Rose Inserra

PM Plus

Ruby Level 28

U.S. Edition © 2013 HMH Supplemental Publishers
10801 N. MoPac Expressway
Building #3
Austin, TX 78759
www.hmhsupplemental.com

Text © 2003 Cengage Learning Australia Pty Limited
Illustrations © 2003 Cengage Learning Australia Pty Limited
Originally published in Australia by Cengage Learning Australia

9   1957   14
19253

Text: Rose Inserra
Printed in China by 1010 Printing International Ltd

Acknowledgments
Photographs by: AAP, p. 15 left and right; ANT Photo Library/K. Griffiths, p. 9 bottom /NHPA, p. 17 top; Australian Picture Library/Corbis, pp. 9 top, 17 bottom /Minden Pictures, pp. 19, 13 bottom; AUSCAPE, p. 31 bottom left /C. Andrew Herley, p. 12 /C. Andrews, p. 14 /Davo Blair, p. 27 bottom /Graham Roberston, p. 16 /Greg Harold, p. 18 top /Hellio-Van Ingen, p. 10 top /Jean-Paul Ferrero, p. 20 bottom /Joe McDonald, p. 13 top /Nicholas Birks, p. 11 /Ralph Ginzburg-Peter Arnold, front cover, p. 10 bottom; Bill Thomas, pp.8, 30, 31 top left and right and bottom right; Coo-ee Picture Library, pp. 5 top and bottom, 28; Getty Images, p. 6 bottom; Lee Walker, pp. 1, 24; Lochman Transparencies/Brett Denis, p. 18 bottom; Newspix, pp. 22, 23, 26, 27 top; Photolibrary.com/Index Stock, pp. 2, 6 top, 32; Scancolor, p. 25; Still Pictures, p. 29; Stock Photos, pp. 4, 7, 20 top, 21, 28 top.

Wildlife in the City
ISBN 978 0 75 786912 9

Contents

Chapter 1
Changing Habitats

Our environment is always changing. Sometimes people clear land for building cities, towns, and farms. As the population of a city grows, more land is cleared for houses and **industry**. People bring **exotic** animals and plants to these areas, which were once the **habitat** of many kinds of native wildlife and plants.

A new housing development

When people change or destroy habitats, many animals **adapt** to the changes by finding other places to live. Towns and cities — even your own backyard — can provide alternative habitats. Buildings, parks and gardens, swimming pools, ponds, and fountains supply wildlife with their basic needs: food, water, shelter, and protection from **predators**.

It is important to protect the natural environment and native wildlife, but we can also share our cities with animals. What animals live around you? Go outside, sit quietly, and watch. You will soon see!

Chapter 2

Birds

If you go for a walk in any city in the world, you will probably see two types of common birds: pigeons and sparrows.

Pigeons

In the wild, pigeons live on cliff faces or in grasslands, and build their nests in the cracks and ledges of cliffs. In towns and cities, skyscrapers and bridges provide ideal nesting places, while window ledges and **eaves** of roofs are good places to shelter.

In their natural habitat, pigeons feed on grain and seeds. In towns and cities, they can be found around wharves, railway yards, grain **silos,** and wherever there is grain. They also feed on food scraps and handouts from people. Fountains, outdoor faucets, water sprinklers, and ponds all provide water.

Pigeons breed several times a year. In the wild, their natural predators are hawks, falcons, and eagles, but in cities and **urban** areas, cats are their main predator. With the constant supply of food, and fewer predators, pigeon populations thrive in some cities.

? DID YOU KNOW?

In cities with large pigeon populations, statues and buildings need to be cleaned constantly.

Sparrows

Some sparrows feed on seeds and grains in open fields, but many sparrows have moved into cities where there is plenty of food and shelter. Sparrows eat from bird feeders that people set out and nibble on food scraps.

They rest in shady corners and make their nests by **scavenging** bits of paper, thread, and plastic as well as using some natural nesting materials, such as dry grass and feathers.

Sparrows often make their nests under the eaves of roofs.

A lyrebird

Peregrine falcons

Peregrine falcons are found almost everywhere. They are the fastest animals in the world, flying at around 124 miles per hour.

Their natural habitat is forests, where they nest high in hollow trees or on cliff faces. Sometimes peregrine falcons move into cities. They choose high places to nest, such as the ledges of tall city buildings and power lines.

A peregrine falcon with its chick

? DID YOU KNOW?

People in cities have noticed that some peregrine falcons come back to their favorite nesting places year after year.

Peregrine falcons are raptors, or birds of prey, that feed on small to medium-sized birds. In cities, peregrine falcons hunt and eat small birds, especially pigeons and sparrows. Instead of chasing birds through the air, peregrine falcons dive from above and tackle their prey. The attack is fast and unexpected.

Dangers

City life can be dangerous for peregrine falcons.

- Sometimes their eggs are accidentally knocked down from their nesting sites.
- The air pollution in some cities can make them sick.
- Because they fly so fast, sometimes they don't see power lines and become trapped in them.
- They can be hit by vehicles.

Chapter 3

Bats

Have you ever seen dark shapes, like birds, flying outside at night? Do they make chirping sounds? Chances are you are seeing bats, not birds. Bats are **nocturnal** animals — they fly around in search of food at night, and sleep, or **roost**, upside-down during the day.

In the wild, large **colonies** of bats live in many different habitats, including dark caves, trees, and even deserts.

? DID YOU KNOW?
Bats are the only **mammals** that can fly.

Microbats

Small bats are called microbats. They eat insects and, because they can't see very well in the dark, they use echolocation to find their way around and to hunt and catch prey.

Echolocation

Bats make high-pitched noises as they fly about. When these sounds hit an object, they bounce back to the bat, like an echo. The echoes guide the bat to the object. If it's an insect, the bat will have a tasty dinner. If it's a building or a tree, the bat will avoid flying into it.

Microbats have adapted to living in cities. They roost in warm or protected places, such as in drainpipes, chimneys, and under the eaves of roofs.

Megabats

Large bats are called megabats. They eat fruit, blossoms, and nectar. Fruit bats have large eyes to see in the dark. They have an excellent sense of smell and can find food easily.

Like microbats, megabats have adapted well to life in the city. The bats come in search of food, and the trees in parks and gardens provide the fruit, nectar, and pollen that bats like to eat.

Gray-headed flying foxes are megabats found in Australia. They can be seen during the day in city parks, hanging upside-down from the trees in large colonies. At night they fly to other trees to eat the blossoms and fruits.

? DID YOU KNOW?

Over recent years, people have planted more of the trees that bats like to feed on. This has led to the growth of large bat populations.

Bat colonies to be moved

A large colony of fruit bats, up to 8000, has been roosting in the Botanical Gardens. Their roosting has damaged treetops and stripped branches bare of fruit and leaves. Some important trees and plants have even been destroyed.

The idea is that bats attract other bats, so the bats at the Botanical Gardens will visit the captured bats, where they will also be caught and put into an aviary.

A bat aviary

The Gardens' management has decided that moving the bats is the only way to save precious trees. A new location with suitable habitat has been found in the eastern suburbs, some distance from the Botanical Gardens. Several hundred bats will be captured and kept in an **aviary** at their new home.

The relocation will continue until there are enough bats for a large colony. When the bats are released, experts say that they should stay in their new habitat. This is a new approach to managing wildlife in the city.

Chapter 4

Foxes and Coyotes

Foxes and coyotes can be found everywhere in our cities and towns. They have adapted well to city life because they can eat almost anything and live almost anywhere.

In their natural habitat, foxes and coyotes live in wooded areas, and coastal and semi-desert areas. In the wild, foxes and coyotes feed on whatever they can find, including smaller animals like mice, rabbits, and lizards as well as insects, fruits, and vegetables.

? DID YOU KNOW?

Foxes have a very keen sense of hearing. A red fox can hear a mouse squeak over 100 feet away.

In the city, foxes and coyotes are usually seen in the evening or early in the morning as they scavenge food scraps from garbage cans, or hunt and eat small creatures.

During the day, foxes and coyotes rest in quiet, dark places, such as under houses or thick bushes, in scrap yards, sheds, and deserted buildings.

This fox rests in a scrap metal yard.

Chapter 5

Frogs

Frogs belong to a group of animals called **amphibians**. Frogs live all over the world in a variety of habitats such as swamps, rain forests, creeks, and lakes.

Frogs spend a lot of their time in water, so they are very sensitive to water pollution.

? DID YOU KNOW?

Frogs don't swallow water, they absorb it through their skin. They also absorb oxygen through their skin.

People have destroyed many natural frog habitats by cutting down forests and draining wetlands to build cities and vacation resorts.

Frogs have had to find other habitats, such as garden ponds, creeks, waterways, and backyards, which bring them into close contact with people.

Dangers

Living close to people can be dangerous for frogs.

- Water pollution is dangerous for frogs. There are many ways that water can become polluted. If not disposed of properly, all of the following things can get washed down drains and end up in our waterways:
  - oils from cooking, cars, and industry
  - fuel, paints, cigarette butts, and garden pesticides
  - soap, detergent, and grease from washing cars in the streets
  - paper and plastic packaging, cans, unwanted fishing line, and litter
- Introduced animals that feed on tadpoles can wipe out frog populations in ponds and lakes.

Cane toads were introduced to Australia to eat cane beetles, but the toads have spread across the country, taking over frog habitats and feeding on tadpoles.

19

Chapter 6

Raccoons

Raccoons live throughout North America and are known for their masked face and ringed tail. In the wild, raccoons make their homes in hollow logs or trees. They usually hunt for food at night and sleep during the day. They eat a variety of things including crayfish, frogs, fish, acorns, birds' eggs, corn, fruit, nuts, and mice.

Because raccoons eat such a variety of things, they have easily adapted to life in the city and suburbs. Here they will help themselves to any food source left outside, including garbage cans, bird feeders, gardens, and ponds with fish. Raccoons that find enough food in one area will want to move in. They see a chimney as being similar to a hollow tree. They will also nest in an attic, crawl space, or under a deck or porch.

Although raccoons are cute, they are wild animals and will bite and can be quite dangerous. You should not approach them or feed them. If you see a raccoon during the day, it is probably ill or injured. Leave it alone and notify an adult.

? DID YOU KNOW?

To encourage raccoons that are nesting in or around your house to leave, put a lit flashlight in the area along with a radio playing a talk station loudly.

Chapter 7

Kangaroos

Different cities throughout the world have their own unique wildlife situations. For example, kangaroos are found only in Australia and New Guinea.

Kangaroos like open forest or grassland habitats. At dusk or early morning, large groups of kangaroos, called mobs, feed mostly on grass. Some mobs contain up to fifty kangaroos. During the middle of the day, kangaroos rest or sleep in the shade. At night they search for more food.

Kangaroos lose their natural habitat as cities grow and more land is cleared for building roads or housing estates. They hop off in search of suitable food and territory. While kangaroos don't live in big cities, they can be found roaming at the outskirts. They like large open, grassy areas such as parks, golf courses, and playgrounds. When food is scarce, they move closer to urban areas to feast on leftover food scraps.

But kangaroos can sometimes hop into dangerous situations, such as across roads, or into yards where dogs might attack them.

Chapter 8

Penguins and Seals

In many countries, large numbers of people live along the coast. They use the sea for many things, including transportation, fishing, and recreation.

Penguins and seals are **marine** animals that also spend time out of the water. On land, they can come into contact with people. Sometimes penguins and seals establish colonies close to busy cities.

People have built special platforms where seals can rest in the sun.

Little Penguins

Little penguins, also called fairy penguins, are the smallest of all penguins. They can be found in Australia and New Zealand. Little penguins are birds, but they cannot fly. At sea, the penguins' natural predators are seals, sharks, and killer whales.

At dusk, little penguins come on land to lay their eggs in burrows on sand dunes or among rocks. If the penguins nest close to towns, dogs, foxes, rats, and cats also prey on them.

? DID YOU KNOW?

In some places, people can watch penguins come ashore without disturbing them. Tourists come to see the penguins walk up the beach to their burrows.

People try to protect the nesting sites of little penguins. They are fenced off so people can't walk through and disturb the eggs or the young penguins. In some areas, roads that penguins frequently cross are closed at night so they can cross safely.

Penguins in Sweaters

My Vacation Journal

Saturday

Today we went for a walk on the beach. We found many little penguins covered in sticky, black oil. Mom ran back to the hotel to tell someone, while Dad and I waited on the beach.

A wildlife ranger named Kelly and some volunteer rescuers soon arrived. Kelly said that an oil tanker must have leaked oil into the sea, and that the penguins would be taken to the animal hospital to have the oil cleaned off them. Kelly said we could come and visit them later.

This afternoon when we went to the animal hospital, we saw many penguins being washed. We were also amazed to see penguins wearing little sweaters. Kelly said that some of the penguins were too **stressed** to be washed, so they were given little knitted sweaters to wear. The sweaters stop the penguins from cleaning themselves. If the penguins were left to clean themselves, they would swallow the poisonous oil stuck to their feathers.

We are going back to the hospital on Friday.

Friday

Today was the last day of our vacation, but I wasn't sad. I was really excited because we were going back to visit the penguins at the animal hospital.

It was fantastic to see all the penguins looking so clean and healthy. Some were being fed tiny fish called pilchards.

Kelly took us to see some other penguins in a special swimming pool. She said that after the penguins are cleaned, they are put in this pool for a swim. Then the rescuers check the soft feathers close to the penguins' bodies. If the feathers have stayed dry, the penguins are ready to go back to the sea.

Today was great — the penguins looked so cute and most of them are ready to go home. Kelly has a great job — I'd like to be a wildlife ranger when I grow up.

Seals

Seals depend on the sea for food. Their natural predators are killer whales and sharks, but other threats to seals come from pollution and humans.

Some seals live in harbors close to people; others live in shallow **estuaries** and near sandbars and beaches.

Female seals bring their pups to shore if sharks are feeding nearby. They also come to shore to rest or if the seas are too rough.

 DID YOU KNOW?

Seals can be friendly animals that are not shy of humans. Sometimes people feed seals and they return regularly to get easy meals.

Dangers

Humans cause many dangers to penguins and seals.

Penguins and seals:

- can get tangled in or swallow plastic garbage that ends up in our seas.
- can get trapped in fishing nets.
- can run out of food when waters are over-fished by people.
- can get sick or die from oil spills and chemical pollution washed into the sea.
- can have their breeding and other behaviors disturbed by tourists.

Chapter 9

Helping City Wildlife

Many animals have adapted well to living in cities. Others, especially native wildlife, are struggling to cope with loss of habitat, pollution, and competition from introduced animals.

However, wildlife can be protected and enjoyed by us all. Our backyards, schoolyards, and parks can be turned into "wildlife-friendly" habitats. Here are some things that you can do to help.

Dispose of all garbage thoughtfully. Small animals can get trapped in empty bottles and cans. Plastic rings from drink packs can choke wildlife.

Provide clean water for the wildlife in your backyard.

Create a pond for frogs in your backyard.

Plant trees and grasses that attract local wildlife.

More things you can do

- Keep all garbage cans closed.
- Use natural **pesticides** in your garden.
- Keep cats and dogs inside at night.
- Build nesting boxes for birds and small tree-dwelling animals.

Build piles of small logs and twigs to attract lizards and bugs.

Glossary

adapt — change to fit new surroundings

amphibians — animals that spend part of their life in water and part on land

aviary — a large cage for birds

botanical — to do with the scientific study of plants

colonies — groups of animals living together

eaves — the edge of the roof that extends past the walls

estuaries — wide mouths of rivers where they meet the sea

exotic — not native to an area

habitat — a place where an animal usually lives

industry — when goods are produced in factories and warehouses

mammals — animals that give birth to live young and feed them milk

marine — of the sea or oceans

nocturnal — sleeps in the day and is active at night

pesticides — chemical sprays used to kill insects

predators — animals that hunt and eat other animals for food

roost — a place for resting, sitting, or staying

scavenging — searching for and taking scraps

silos — towers for storing large amounts of grain

stressed — upset and exhausted

urban — in a town or city